Sightseer in This Killing City

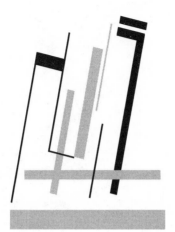

Sightseer in This Killing City

EUGENE GLORIA

PENGUIN POETS

PENGUIN BOOKS
An imprint of Penguin Random House LLC
penguinrandomhouse.com

Pages 95–96 constitute an extension of the copyright page.

LIBRARY OF CONGRESS CATALOGING-IN-PUBLICATION DATA
Names: Gloria, Eugene, author.
Title: Sightseer in this killing city / Eugene Gloria.
Description: New York : Penguin Books, [2019] | Series: Penguin poets
Identifiers: LCCN 2018055871 (print) | LCCN 2018057630 (ebook) |
    ISBN 9780525505648 (ebook) | ISBN 9780143133841 (paperback)
Subjects: | BISAC: POETRY / American / Asian American. | POETRY /
    American / General.
Classification: LCC PS3557.L6485 (ebook) | LCC PS3557.L6485 A6 2019 (print) |
    DDC 811/.54—dc23
LC record available at https://lccn.loc.gov/2018055871

Printed in the United States of America
10 9 8 7 6 5 4 3 2 1

Set in Perpetua Std
Designed by Elyse J. Strongin, Neuwirth & Associates

Contents

Sightseer in This Killing City

[Saudade]

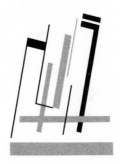

IMPLICIT BODY

Of my self-creation is this legend
of my betrayals, my disloyalty to my origins.

Of my once and future past,
            of rajas and gilded palaces,
of brown sailors building empires, I lay no claim.

      I lay no claim to your founding fathers,
no claim to pearl divers and tattooed pirates
jumping ship to grow a colony in Louisiana.

What I've inherited is this feeding frenzy
            for rainbow, rainbow, rainbow,
this multigenerational spectral light show

inducing a diarrhea of bullets; and no arrests.
I'm the youngest son of a youngest son,
            a second baseman in the minor leagues,

a family trope deputized to react
            and bleed—whose only compensation
is his own capacious longing.

Hand me your gun, America,
            and let my body be the soundtrack
to the spectacle of our recent events.

      If only this miasmic island of sundown
towns and Bible colleges, of folksy neighbors

with their *hiya doin'* gestures and holding
         keys to the kingdom come raining down
with molten rocks upon this megalomania

of abandoned cities, of cowslip turnips, of holy
         JesuschildrenofAmerica, of thee I sing!

Call me Mr. Gone / who's done made / some other plans.
All that remains is nostalgia
         and this aching torso of blue.

THE PALL OF A PAST WORLD

I dreamt of Ornette Coleman six months before he died.
In his apartment a calendar. It read *1978*.
Many bad things happened then, like the killings in city hall:
the mayor and a supervisor
both gunned down by another politician who felt discarded
like the way things were heading in 1978.
Children, many of them from the city, drank the Kool-Aid
laced with cyanide in Guyana that year,
the year I celebrated my birthday at a strip club downing
Seagram's Seven-and-Sevens
in Los Angeles with Ray and Simon.
Had I known grief better and looked at it dead in the eye
it would've been just another fly
desperate between the curtains and the window's glass.
In 1978 I learned for the first time
that dying is something people have to live through.
In sleep, I'm holding my breath
because I'm deep inside the sea. A dreamy divagation
is what Bishop said,
which in theory explains all the commotion in my bed.
When the entire house is still asleep,
I'll be sitting in the back of a pickup with someone
telling me that the land
on either side is a soft blanket of eiderdown.
Even when I slip and fall
headlong in the fields—a falling much like sleep.
I look at my hands all covered in dirt.

How can anyone distinguish waking from dreaming,
sleep from dusk, presence from my hand?
My hand says drive. Which hand, you ask. The big hand
that says it's almost seven.

ZONES OF CONTACT

I. *Saudade*

Baudelaire wrote that the only way to inhabit the present is to revisit it in a work of art. "Go to Europe," my runaway sister whispered in my ear. My sister, who later landed her dream job as a flight attendant, bought me a ticket from SFO to Heathrow. Having graduated to the present, I found myself on a flight deadheading to unemployment. [*Exit above.*] Language is an inadequate vessel. Take the word *saudade,* which comes from a land of shipbuilders and navigators. Say it within the context of empire long gone, of important battles depicted on ceramic and tile. I traveled by rail on the continent. And on the slowest train in the world, I went for two whole days from Paris to Lisbon.

II. *Supertramp*

Twenty years later, I am taking a train in northern Spain to see in person how ceramics inform Frank Gehry's design of the Guggenheim in Bilbao. Imagine a set of functionless bowls in the rain. [*Enter several strange Shapes.*] Twenty years earlier, I was running away from a pint-sized case of heartbreak. I thought I was going to stoke an old flame, a German classmate I met in Jacob Needleman's religion class at SF State U. She was a potter. Her work verging on the impractical, I first thought. I had a standing invitation to visit her in Hamburg. She was an ideal host when I did. She put me up for a couple nights, and I had hopes of staying longer. But her square roommate, who loved, *loved* Supertramp, was growing impatient with a guest she didn't invite. Who could blame her? I was a bum. Her profound admiration for the song "Breakfast in America" was a testament to her world of disembodied arrivals. Imagine a nagging ringtone in a darkened theater whenever that song comes on the radio. The roommate's irritation with my visit crystallized when my Hamburg host introduced me to her new boyfriend. The Libyan boyfriend she met on the train.

III.   *Santa Apolónia Station*

I want to believe that *saudade* has something to do with arrival, a pause that lingers like homesickness for a place where you've never been, or the difference in the equation between arrival and departure. And if you round out all my miscalculations, my bad math might end up with a fraction of burnt flesh from my hobo heart. Oh, loveless me, *O sole mio, yada, yada.* I was in my twenties, brimming with unnecessary drama. *Saudade?* No. I know it now. *Saudade* is a progeny of music, a wayward emotion that slips into wordlessness, a thing of *AnOther* culture. [*Burden, dispersedly within.*] And if *saudade* is only a feeling, then it must be the only thing that keeps me moving——. The sonorous grind of the potter's wheel, hands shaping clay from memory, that momentary catch in the throat.

IV.   *[Enter Song.]*

I heard a composer explain that in opera, when dialogue suddenly shifts into overdrive, emotions are climbing toward a heightened moment of arrival when spoken words are simply not enough. After two whole days of not speaking, I heard a small human hand tap on my door. It was the innkeeper's daughter holding a tray of coffee, hard bread with jam and butter. The coffee came in a cup and saucer, but it was her nervous gaze I recall, and her skin smooth as a celadon vase. I laugh now, recalling my volcanic excitement for her chore of delivering my breakfast, which I regarded as a supreme act of kindness. I must have frightened her with my gestures of gratitude. She was only a child with her white socks and Mary Janes. I blurted the only word I knew in Portuguese, *obrigado*, I said over and over again, *obrigado*, before she left the room without a word.

APRON

Unlike the grotesque bonnet
worn at church, the apron
is more a second cousin
to the humble scarf in winter.
The apron would never say
"So what" to you. She's agreeable
as a kitchen mantle with ripening fruit.
A sponge when it comes to stink:
splatter of fish scales and fish guts,
the errant strafe of grease
from angry skillets, the teary onion's
grief and stutter. In middle life,
the apron aspires to stand before
sinners and saints and carve
verses on stone: *Mon coeur mis à nu*,
she'll tattoo on your chest.
She's your last line of defense
against burnt anchovies,
the wide net draping
over the frightful forest,
the canvas cradling the boxer's face,
a makeshift dressing
on a playground wound.
The apron is the fulsome embrace
for a brother shoving off—
the one with empty pockets
coming home to the damp, dark
folds of her familiar stink.

LINER NOTES FOR MONK

"Monk's Mood" [false start]

I got off the bus too soon before my stop, so I had to walk a few blocks in order to regain my bearings. Thelonious Monk said, "It's always night / or we wouldn't need light." I read this in an essay. I wanted to have a conversation with someone to lighten my load. I remember seeing a woman disembarking from the next bus. Our gazes locked for a long second. [*It is always night wherever you go.*]

"Crepuscule with Nellie" [breakdown]

[*Monk continues alone and quiet.*] Northward leads to the river, southward back to my hotel room. An entire week had passed and I hadn't exchanged seven words with another human. The sound of words directed at me felt like a hand on my shoulder, an arm brushing against my skin. It is always night when silence overcomes me, silence opening up within me like a wound. Black keys, I've been told, have an ominous, mysterious sound.

"Misterioso"

[*Monk conversing with water.*] What we end up making, whether it's something we do by ourselves or with others, is always a form of conversation. My presence is solid, but others see me as a fishing weir, a foamless Mister So-and-So, a scavenger for anything that would flatter his eyes. What I want is a garden that will not perish, a bed of imperial white peonies.

NIGHTHAWKS OCEANIA

In a city of loners men in suits
hunker over bowls of ramen.
You must forgive my useless glimpses,
to draw conclusions would be unfair.

They're taking up room.
Our ramen bar an extension domicile
between time off and work time.
What Hopper saw in his American city

is my version of elemental awe.
Night and no one to pass judgment.
I'm here with my bosses, dear Monk,
dear Coltrane. We're happy and unfound.

Take this colored sheet of paper and fold it
in the prescribed creases, then pull out a bird,
a solitary vireo, a swan, no, a woman
turned into a swan and a god in hot pursuit.

I want Monk to stop spinning like a lonely planet,
I want Coltrane to assure us that we're an island—
that we're the night and also the ocean.

THE MONK'S TALE

With razor-creased trousers a barber
visits Ninna-ji Temple in sakura season.
        Standing by a squat *omuro* tree, the barber
is approached by an old man who
        recognizes him & commences to recount

a tale about a monk murdered
        long ago exactly where he's standing.
The old man's swollen lips bud
        into contusions, reminding
the barber of delft ceramic plates,
        or the domed ceiling of a mosque.

He is tasting the best part of cheese,
        blue & sharp, a dewy god's pale raiment.
The iridescent blue of a common grackle,
        suburban skies, the blue Jesus in Cologne,
a scent, a gulf, a mood in Iceland,
        or things demarcating distance, an end
point to a path, a bottle of gin, blue.
        The barber in abeyance listens until
the old man says that *he* died here

        at this spot. The barber hands him
his camera & poses for a picture
        of him standing upright, smart
as an ampersand & the *omuro*
        tree, a canopy of white blossoms,
drapes over slim-waisted silhouettes.

.13.

THE WAR ON DRUGS

On your way to leave me, / idiots turned heads of state. / You left a keepsake on my bed, / what turned out to be an empty box / wrapped in bright orange foil. / I settled for violets instead of furs, / bartered vinegar and salt for your insurgents. / The war on drugs is an entire season of camo-wear. / The war on drugs is acting / upon all your irrational fears. / The war on drugs is an eye for an eye. / The war on drugs is all fun and games until someone loses an eye. / The war on drugs is an interruption of being. / The war on drugs is fleeing / even when it isn't your nature to flee. / The war on drugs is about a country / with low self-esteem. / The war on drugs is / being on the good side of bad. / The war on drugs is hurling / your broken placenta jars through space. // The war on drugs is sorry / for everything turning into tumbleweeds / rolling over the inky waves. / The war on drugs is never having to say you're sorry. / The war on drugs is a gust, / a sparrow's beating wing. / The war on drugs is a husband / who wants a new car. / The war on drugs is a wife with expensive taste. / Whom do you fear? / The war on drugs is believing / that you're not / in the midst of the war on drugs. / The war on drugs is a blues song. / The war on drugs is a blues song / with a white, hot organ solo. / The war on drugs is about brutalist architecture. // The war on drugs is / engulfed in crimson petals. / The war on drugs is seeing / yourself in the crosshairs / while setting your sights on me. / The war on drugs will be aired on your local TV. / The war on drugs is a Broadway musical. / The war on drugs is a mobilization of absolutes. / The war on drugs is a piece of cake. / The war on drugs is / my best Palmer Method penmanship looping / in horizontal rows across the page. / The war on drugs is / reciting the proletarian verse of daisies. / The war on drugs is looking / at the unremarkable sea, / and you, love, never looking back.

THE SHAPE OF

1.

His real name

I have been told

came from

weeds and

peons.

They say

his cold eyes,

circulars or folders,

traveled through

the Caraguá.

2.

My interlocutor

disclosed a secret.

I will tell you

of my comrades,

their destiny

was, I suspect,

circular towers and

nation.

[A Walled City of Psalms]

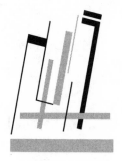

THIRTEEN DREAMS AND ONE DUTERTE

[Number 1 Dream]

A wall diademed with broken glass
        can tear the skin
of anyone who dares to scale the wall

Hot box for a house, a tinderbox of electric fans
        I took to walking in my sleep to
streets with no hills which snaked for miles

[Number 2 Dream]

Open sewage like a babbling brook of tar

[Number 3 Dream]

Duterte is a verb as in "to be Duterted" or
to be body-bagged, to be hunted as in a dream

[Number 4 Dream]

Outside our compound
        we roamed the streets like dogs
Dogs were aliens among aliens

They came of age and began
        distrusting us
Our lives lived below sea level

[Number5Dream]

Ubiquitous as smoke, we squinted our eyes
      squeezing long hits from our smokes
At dusk our hair was drenched in it

Lips glistening with grease
Strays didn't stand much of a chance with us

[Number6Dream]

The silent *g* in *poignant*
      confounds our guild
Failure bestowed upon us like a gift
      The law knocking at our domicile—

without probable cause
      The law would never surrender evidence
when asked directly

[Number7Dream]

The street is so congested
      it's an extrajudicial killing
Manila is so deafening it's practically soundproof

[Number8Dream]

The nature of dreams is to affirm our forced
      disappearance   Duterte's streets
before the typhoon   I am
      a typhoon transnationalizing

.20.   across the archipelago, a balikbayan
      box in a loaded warehouse They call me loadie

[Number9Dream]

I am an Overseas Foreign Worker, someone's *kuya*
      your *lola*, your auntie Librada, your Liberty
of Strangers, your domestic, a helper

[Number10Dream]

Above the pile of stink and vermin, a bell tower
      where a hammer strikes
Bong Bong, the cruel strain of our cultural legacy

[Number11Dream]

I am 10:30 in the morning, a kali stick fighter
      demonstrating a knife attack   I am a demo
mon confrère in a kicking conference

[Number12Dream]

I hear whispers rustling through the pampas
      a tone-deaf priest
trying to keep up with the choir

[Number13Dream]

My two balikbayan boxes opened without a sound
      no different from two black stones that reach far

[Number14Dream]

I've learned to bark in another language   .21.
      at the dark I'm meant to watch

WHY THEY BEES THAT WAY

Be not the man with a compass in the forest primeval
      or the highway lacquered with ice
Be not the expedition darkened by sickness
      or the man with a mission, or the man with a plan

Be not the cat who's strapped
      or the nanny dressed to the nines
Be not the open-carry goon robbed of his gun
      or the boa on the branch that will not hold

Be not the death of lilacs
      or the Chinese market collapse
Be not the screw, the pseudo-dad
      or the stabilizing father

Be not the beauty measured by the utterance of men
      or the boar in the hunting lodge ready for the feast
Be not the obdurate peasant in the shoemaker's shop
      or the core faculty, the *Mayflower*, or the Plymouth Rock

Be not the story often told
      or the shot heard round the world
Be not the pleasing perpetrator working the room
      or the melodramatic knife, or the meanness in irony

Be not the wild, or the peaceable one
      Be not the knife peeling an onion
or the shepherd boy rendered into a song
      Be not the elegy that turned
into anaphora of my irrefutable truths

Be not the hour's brave splendor, or the dream
        of peaches in a lonely kitchen in July
Be not the sap, be not the sapling, be not
        the tree, but the root that inhales the dirt
Be the dirt, be the *dirt* that knows the taste of air

Be not the air, but the bee-loud glade
        Be not the honey in Stevens's concupiscent curd
Be not the curd, but the tar, be not
        the sentence sense, but the broken syntax
Be not the bold propulsive, or the black lung of coal
        be the black, be the sound in your locomotive soul

THE MAID

Before she let her go not a speck of dirt
Sullied her bleached blouse except for the dark
Rope of hair she sometimes coiled into
A tidy bun with beaded sweat gracing the
Mandarin collar and a pressed hanky the sun
Lurking so the hanky became both veil and
Rag unlike her skirt a bloomful
Tent for tiny boys cooling with scent of sea air

Air rifling through the trees and
Bloomful sheets with camisoles on the line
And the flag flutter warning of forbidden zones
Sun scorching the grass into oaken fields
The yard where we hunted dragonflies well
Into dinnertime or thereabouts until
Dark I suppose or when rain fell—Whatever
Dirt or blemish upon her name only my mother knew

THE HOLLER

I'm opening up & then shutting down
      Why this compulsion to tell everyone
when I should keep it zipped

Why tattle to the dentist who expects
      nothing more than good hygiene
Why, oh why, tell the manicurist

& her blind husband typing in braille
      to his pretty cousin Thuy
who read my lips & sang

Why is he bothering us with this
      Grateful for dreams, I dreamt of my sister
wearing a chador & living in Kansas

I must write her a note of glad tidings
      with tidbits of nostalgia instead of our grief
Death, she learned, is an accomplishment

a wafer of sun the sky took for Communion
      & the labor of water is transforming
the human body into spittle in the wind

The keep, the culvert, the crawl space
      the circular breathing, the water phone
the mother dead, dear dead

How remote the spirit feels this finale
      How best to submit my thesis as my final final
Acknowledging that my mother is done, kaput

Let's not get cross, I tell her. Let's get pissed
        Celebrate all that's still wet in Kansas
Is that OK with you? Two of us sailing along

among the drones locked in their labors
        Maybe we're all in need of pampering
My students, poor saps, feeling sentimental

about leaving this old place for the known world
        I envy them for the promises they keep
the rebel holler they harbor in their hearts

Who wouldn't want to be them
        seasick, uncompassed sailors

KING LEAR

I wanted to be him, that fly old dude
breaking into tears in front of our class,
reading a passage from *King Lear*.
I'd be making it up if I told you
exactly which part of the play it was,
but we had just started the tragedies
and *Lear* was tops in his charts.
What I do remember is the swank
Gucci loafers he wore,
the blue cashmere V-neck sweater
over his creased wool pants.
He shopped at Wilkes Bashford,
which catered more to the hip patrician
than to this lit prof at SF State.
What made him so endearing
was not his tradecraft nor elocution.
Oh, sure, Shakespeare is cool
and he can make a grown man cry.
But did his shoes have discernible flair?
I may not be the sharpest blade
in the drawer, but I took away
something from his class,
which is more than what I can say
about our lumberjack profs.
On my birthday Susie Asado bought me
a Hermès belt with that bitchin' H logo.
Neither a witty fool nor a foolish wit
but more like that fly guy who's able
to leap tall buildings in a single bound.

IN LANGUEDOC

On Rue de l'Aiguillerie, formerly the Cami Romieu
        where St. Roch was arrested as a spy,
only the immigrant workers are up at this hour

and I am bookworming——.
        What a perfect companion my poet would make
for my lonely trek to Carcassonne, a hilltop

        fortress of the Cathars, slaughtered
by the crusading armies of the Holy See
        who had designs for their homeland,

blood-soaked soil founded by the Visigoths
        and centuries later inhabited by the Cathars
with their gouged-out eyes as if their enemies

                were only switching off their hallway light.
It's cold out, though the shit-flecked streets
        are now awash with couples holding hands,

a city of words in the full bloom of immense arousal.
                In Languedoc I dream of a gated community,
though I have yet to crash that party.

Like every other word in French a new gate opens——
        an inward place my poet takes me to

that door to a river, which is a secret
dwelling for all our unheralded feelings.

Of absence and erasure, the Cathars
                    must have seen themselves
roiling toward an inner sea.

                I imagine St. Marie of Egypt,
who suddenly decides to take up
                    swimming when all her life

she's known only the desert. And the sun
            hasn't moved from my shuttered windows,
a faint shadow of some distant tree,

            St. Marie's mortification of the flesh
must be that distant trembling thing
                    on the building's northeast wall.

I am St. Roch, a spy of my own undoing,
            arriving on the shores of Languedoc. Wounded
pilgrim, you are home.

SETTLING ON A BED IN THE GOON REPUBLIC

There was nowhere else to be but in bed
with you who wears her tiredness well.
We'll retire for chitchat, substitute the beds
in our dorm rooms for capsule beds in love
motels with rooms adorned with frescoes
of saints over a congregation of souls—
our bed, a congress fevered with ghosts
of skin, hands, our fluid stains, a bed alit
in this goon republic where our commander
has declared our eyes, our seeing, a capital
offense; a semaphore flag for public unrest.
Your hip against mine, your limbs to my lips
like on our first parting at the campus rally
where we sealed what parting cancels.

THE SUITCASE

after Gabriel García Márquez

Once a man traveled from Manila
To Rome, toting his dead daughter
In a Samsonite suitcase hoping
For an audience with the pope.

Her body the odor of tidy linens.
Her skin maintained its olive glow.
He took her out as if unpacking
A Stradivarius or laying down

A lily of the valley on the settee.
The settee in the hotel where he was
Installed was green-and-yellow paisley.
He owned a tie in that pattern—

Ties inside a case with other ties,
Shoehorned boots in velvet sacks.
But where he was welcome most
Was often where he was his worst.

Grander than most, his suitcase
Once held the sultan of Brunei,
Desolate and cursing his handlers
Who knew he was good to go.

Another time he smuggled a modest
Booty of Poussin's paintings, a bust
Of Diderot. A mighty, mighty
Fortress, a walled city of psalms

And shrapnel was his only reward.
Like Darwish's country of words,
He was in search of land to speak in.
Neither miracles nor blessings

Were made available for the man
Wishing more for his daughter
Beyond passing freely through
The customhouse of heaven.

No grief was greater for a parent
Whose fate it was to outlive his child.
Stranger to light cargo, he became
A bearer of islands, an entire archipelago.

MY PHANTOM ESCORT, PIER PAOLO PASOLINI

The historical cry

electric

vegetal

green as billiards

plush

engulfed

the Tiber

Behind

Monteverde

little shoeboxes

the putrid-

green Tiber

bathed

with sanatoriums

IN THE ANDES

In the Andes where I've never been
they don ponchos woven like breathable bath mats
        and women and men with long hair
wear bad lids, a cross between cowboy
        and bowler hats. In the Andes they blow
on reed pipes which are really handheld
        church organs and there, full of faces
hail as in Sunday Mass singing songs of lambs
                full of yearning and remembering
their twenties in Madrid at the Plaza Mayor.
        Thank you and sorry, thank you and well
thank you again for believing the possible all
                like a little river in a hurry to arrive
toward some place that is a happy mystery
        from where I stand. I am sorry for disliking
nature poetry and sorry for not liking little children
        bragging I've played this I've played this
I've played this I've played this until they're shushed
        by a silver-haired librarian who is me in a fable,
O me who is just a feather in an Andean hat,
                a little minnow in your clever pond.

[*And the sheen of their spears was like stars on the sea*

—Lord Byron]

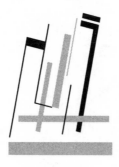

SIGHTSEER IN THIS KILLING CITY

Contagion smiles wide as elevator doors
you enter with a crop of pubic curls on your head.
My cousin is lit like a Georges de La Tour canvas—

        she, a lumen prepubescent, a thread
of smoke spiraling from a thin cigarette.

Old photo she saved so you won't forget.
    There are territories of memory we have yet
to explore with creased maps, lamps, torches—

refugios for sightseers in this killing city.
    Come daylight when I awake, Dallas
will still be dark but for the sound light brings,

a mad rumble of boxcars bearing goods
    for the red states of North America.

When I arrived, I saw the grassy knoll
down that killing square. My cousin sick
and so I came with only Roethke's line:
    "On things asleep, no balm."

Her nurse explains, of which I know,
    half of it untrue: "The body runs a motor
with a shutoff valve when in crisis mode.

    It finds a way to fix itself."
My cousin's motor hums in sleep,
driving further into a hint of spring.

And tomorrow is the past,
    a gurney's wheels squeaking
dry and violent through contagious halls.

NURSE NACIREMA

Not a swimmer in sapphire seas, but only
someone's dad who went out for a pack
of smokes to script his own undoing. Call him

a linguistic ship, which doesn't need
a skipper, a misplaced marine
in a forest of stiletto and swagger.

Welcome to a wilderness of downed timber.
His tree a lit wedding gown—white,
green, yellow, red, then all white again.

In this light, the nurse enters, hair
cut short makes her look butch. Her hem-
line hangs stiffly over daikon legs,

a boxer with a pug nose.
Her provenance is Manileña—
hails from the barrio of Tondo,

and packs a knife in her purse.
She wiped her switchblade with a tissue
and clicked blade back into the handle.

The merchant seaman had scoped out the skirt.
So sayeth the knife telling us her version: *All he wanted*
was to feel good, all he wanted was to talk shoes . . .

He sidled up to the nurse waiting for the bus
when a knife appeared and told him to go to hell.
Down he went into a kaleidoscope of broken mirrors,

a festive flotilla, blood, and pavement.
The seaman doubles over,
then falls flat on the seat of his pants.

On the corner of Haight and Fillmore,
failure drapes his body like an oversized shirt
flowing like jibs in front of Hank's 500.

THE HANDSOME FACE OF TATLONGHARI

Let it be an idea, or a tongue of flame
        over his head. Let it be a Quaker's syntax,
a fragment of inner light. Lead him

to a drawer and the candle he will convene
        with a book of matches and wax melting on
his hands and feet: a boy in shorts
        and slippers on Three Kings marking the end

of Christmas. Tatlonghari will arrive
        years later to nurse his fevered body—

a tree denuded of its ornaments left against
        a pole tall, pockmarked, and creosoted
a lineman scampered up with spiked heels.

He lit the candle on the darkened street,
        the tree's wan branches took a shine
to the tiny flame he held in his hand:

boy with lit candle and scent of burnt pine.
        A needle then a branch and another branch
licked the fire and a moment more the tree

turned into a burning bush and the flames
        grew a face, not the bearded face of Moses,
but more the face of a bearded woman

that was also the handsome face of Tatlonghari
        mouthing "Nice job, G. Now what?"
The pole was charred, but the fire—

the *fire*? No houses burned, the baby pyromaniac
        mute as a glass of water before the tree.
Whenever Tatlonghari worked the piano

he reduced us to weepy violets.
        Loosening the slipknot
and the anchor, he understood what comes
                for us at the end.

A grown-ass man in another country, he saw again
        that tree lit against a storefront window and spied
a nurse through and through at the bus stop

        between Haight and Fillmore where festive
in green, red, and the contradiction of her knife
                against skin, slitting open
what magma or lava this man can hold.

AVE NACIREMA

Baby Nacirema was as dolled up as a jeepney:
a surfeit of bling on the Pacific Coast Highway.
Haunted by the territories we traveled—

you'd think the two of us were husband and wife.
Some regard me as a demon, some as a terror.
So let me be a demon, let me be a reviled thing.

The "Ave Maria" consoles us. I sing it loud—
no, boisterous as a coarse field of rapeseed!
I know my limitations.   I'm only a knife.

When the deed is done and I'm deep
inside you, thinking only one thing—
riding shotgun with Nacirema

        all the way to St. Pete and back.
Our nature is to hold on to what we know:
mine is a story about a woman going down

the National Road clear to the Pacific Ocean.
        That mine is a story forged in fire,
going back to Stockton, California, back

to the Alaskan canneries, back
to a prayer and a man who killed
another man on a merchant ship.

Mine is a story about Magellan whose ship
        compassed the world. Magellan,
whose alliance with Rajah Humabon

dimmed darkly into a cruel song:
And the sheen of their spears
           was like stars on the sea——.

I know what I know and what I know
goes back to the iron-tipped lance
that felled the man. Who could say
she loved me?   *Love me?*

How could a woman love a knife?
Daga, I was called, though Magellan's name
           lived longer than mine.

LIKE THE SPARS OF A SAILING SHIP

Reject the locus of your identity, say *mijo*, say
Shiver me timbers, and welcome with open arms
curses extolling the creak of floorboards.

There's only lyric, the rest is merely prose.
There're only two types of people: those who
slice the world in half and those who don't.

Upstairs in their bed an old couple snore
and their lady bedspacer pretends to sleep.
Stairs and then floorboards begin to titter

and stutter in their outside voice: no one
will say but everyone knows why he came.
In the dark she's willing to open herself up.

T. S. Eliot reading in his timbreless voice:
"There is only the trying. The rest
          is not our business."

North of Edo, in the warlord's house,
the floorboards were made to sing—
blessings upon the arrival of assassins.

SEAMSTRESS TO THE BAND

All the squares, go home! —Sly and the Family Stone

She stands on the bridge in a man suit
        cut and fly, blowing kisses
to the village. Her mama wore a floral apron
        Nacirema could still smell.

At the service, church ladies sang the dry-bone
        psalms she hums to herself.

        Can't run into Sabine and François
coz she'll snare them in a headlock

        and start boo-hooing like a little bitch. Sabine
once kissed her on both cheeks and said, "*Je ne vais*

pas vous oublier." She spits a coin of mucus
        at her mistakes, her blouse filling up

like sails, the nuclear plant fuming
        its stacks, that funerary music, its shadow
of clouds—and broken clay pots behaving
        like unruly charges, leaking daylight through

the narrow apertures of her borrowed coat.
        She is undressing now and folding her suit

and underthings on the curb. The person
she was, was negotiating a temporary truce.
A towel wrapped just above her breast
      when she returned to the curb
where she left her suit, watch, and wallet.

                  A dusting of snow now
covers all her things. Standing
there with her new haircut, her shorn hair.

                                          * * * *

      Rain all in a rush to fall
in Effingham, Illinois
      Lightning spilling in buckets
right through the skylight

Nacirema won't go
      to Lourdes like her mama—
she'll stitch her mistakes and for penance
      walk the Camino in Spain

She's terrified of being dirt, terrified
      of being a perfect equation
Someone said she's in England, in London

or in Paris, France. Rain she tows
      like a carry-on bag—rounding
the horn without any underpants.

THE WAR ON DRUGS

Some fool moons   are sickle shaped—
serving those   who are packing nines.
Whereas at the dojo Baby Nacirema—

                              call her
your *lover boy*—is far removed
from the slinky sea   Now Boot Knife, he

starts talking smack &   Nacirema,
your brown Betty   in thy gun culture,
starts compiling   her all-weather
equipment for   the long haul.

                              Femmes fatales
run the risk of flimsy stratagems
whereas the knife   is nothing
but an adjunct emotion,   a device

in a list she   divvies up
for her second lieutenants: masters
of the slice & dice,   laying down

their burners &   gats & going
to the mattresses.

Nacirema's scowls   are smiles—
the pleasing kind,   letting you know
                    that men are as the time is
& your lover boy is nowhere near.

NE ME QUITTE PAS

a mistranslation of Jacques Brel's song

On a scooter a boy sped by with his girl, and I caught a glimpse
        of you, white as a dispossessed aristocrat,
a puzzle left unsolved. These faces, dark, dark, and inexact
        [doomed assemblies from the sea]
assume that sheen of tropical resorts—
              narcotic blue in banana republics.

    There are no special visas for those who leave their lives
        behind:
lives cast with others, lives freighted with deportation papers.
We of the unmoored,   ships of no destination,

                          mountains reduced
to ashes of final unction—we who find ourselves
        bullied, battered,
            and mispronounced, a caravan
of immigrants picnicking at the side of the road.

Ne me quitte pas, ne me quitte pas—I used to say.
        Nacirema, Nacirema,

I, too, am Nacirema, mother-sister, bride of Nada,
        bride of Void, Nacirema.

    No alien harbors will berth our ships—
we who shall and forever be plankton   for the white whale
    and its yeast of malice.

A MUTINY OF FLOWERS

We sacked three kingdoms in a day for want of flowers
Throats bared, our cries   choked for want of flowers

And there the armies of wandering   assembled
Thirty mighty families   erased for want of flowers

Their prayers sent by carrier pigeons and passing ships
Then we burned their ships, a phantom   fleet of flowers

From their ashes we grew tall churches   by the sea
Crosses high as trees   sprung instead of flowers

We surrendered our gloves, scarves, overcoats, and wallets
Pressed with photos of loved ones   for want of flowers

The empire's affliction is   the stranglehold of lice
If they had a voice, they'd sound like the violence of flowers

The most florid note is kind of blue   we've disguised
As longing, a quiet field   of undetonated flowers

MY SAD ECONOMIST ON THE NATURE OF THINGS

after Picasso's *Deux femmes courant sur la plage*

My sad economist sees the green world as a
menacing, watchful jungle that stinks of defeat—
someone's always got to pony up, she'd say.

Then time and the lonely hour's folded skirt
descended upon her like a strain of unwelcome
occurrences: not clouds opening up like curtains

but the scent of sea and the fishmongers' fresh
catch of monkfish and flounder waylaid her into
a stupor for scallop shells and trails and old faces

spouting their *buen camino* as if there's no mañana.
On the Camino are pokeweeds and *pulpo,* sardines
in tin, stale bread, and a woman named Nacirema

who practiced capoeira and bobbed and weaved
to demonstrate just how she's able to manhandle her.
So it came to pass for every economist

like her to confess their blind spot for anomalies
despite past remonstrations to the contrary.
When the woman named Nacirema returned

to Aix, the world dipped slightly off-kilter:
prices toppled, *X*s and *Y*s tossed about
like mismatched shoes in the bargain rack.

Dow Jones became Love Jones, S&P into TLC.
Even the justices in their dour robes began to err
on the side of volatility; desire fueling the economy.

So an exodus began with bond market traders
and trend analysts; then investment bankers joined
in trickle-down fashion to a gully-washer to Aix,

where happy economists flooded little start-up
communes, cavorting in the praxis of free love
like plus-size women galloping on the beach.

[The Afterlife]

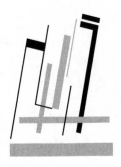

ALFONSO STREET

In Sariaya, Quezon Province, where
            my father's people live, bananas
and mangoes in colored cellophane adorn
            windowsills like gaudy evening wear.
In Botong's pastorals, a fluvial fiesta
            litters Laguna de Bay with lighted
tiny boats like a fleet of candled hopefuls.

Elsewhere, a nervous boy measures his week
            with good days and bad days like innocents
walking on pavements wary of cracks.
            In Caracas, a swarm of bees attacks a boy.
His dog shields his body with its own.
            The boy lives; the dog dies shortly after.

On Alfonso Street, a kid I knew
            is paraded on a wooden wagon
with a matronly woman at the lead.
            My metal trucks with missing wheels
he once coveted. Stateside toys in chipped
            reds and blues I got secondhand
from the children of American GIs.
            His cart with wooden wheels, and rings
round his eyes are gray as metal spokes.
            What good are busted trucks to him
whose brand-name toys are always new?
            Fiesta prince with a shuttlecock crown,
fellow heir of bad blood.

In the kingdom of children where
we conjure angels from rain, a boy's
        will can spin and hitch the earth.
Here my wheel-less truck remains.
        An ashen kid, gray and gilded,
is trundled by his mom in evening wear.

ON THE DEATH MARCH HE SURVIVED

Airing from the archipelago's fragile limb,
      on the lam in the Land of the Morning—
the radio host with a radio voice fires
and then we are live, streaming on the ether—
      sending a shout-out to Baby Nacirema,

Miss Isle of a Thousand Smiles with teeth
      like the pearly whites of the superfly.
The gun mike shoots a blast of hokey salutations
      while an old woman dodders
with the radio on for company.

      She's companioned by a girl employed
from a family in Panay who speaks to her
in the halting deferential dialect which she
      understands. Her staff,

though she doesn't call them that, are *maids*,
      a dysphemism in a postcolonial era within
the firmament of Don M. and Doña H.
      And so it came to pass that those who waited
after them were recast as *helpers*. Helpers to what?

A compound on Don Pedro Street
      where a man bedridden from soldiering
answers to no rank, priest, or pistol, and another
one like him, a retired colonel, self-possessed,
      who never allowed his sons to forget

the Death March he survived
  and the goon republic shadowing his back
and how suffering determined
an aptitude for money.
  The colonel lorded over his alma mater

in the same way I heard my betters
  pronounce ancient names with airy propriety.
Car exhaust chokes the morning air,
smoke from burnt twigs and parchment; the air,
  imperious in its ascent.

The air of empires,
  land of constant burning and radio loud
where the bedridden man known
only to me as *lelong* or *lolo*. *Pensionado*,
  I remember now, was his other name.

The old woman waddles through a river
  of cats, benedictions for the nun
in a floral apron whose kitchen,
a *refugio* for her pilgrim cats. *Lelong* was unaware
  of the cats. Was he asthmatic?

A piano in the parlor no one ever played,
  and a radio blaring with spiky consonants.
Voices that could use a furtive note
  from mewling cats. Music
rarely heard in that house
  but talk as in the old talkies, radio talk
of urgent matters like the hike

in petrol prices and the driver's beef,
a baby mama wailing over her man
splayed on the street from bullets
         spewed from what might as well be

hoses soaking a thirsty patch of lawn.
     The Philippine Constabulary inspects
the bodies like carpenter ants
assessing a trail of poisoned sweet.
     The law investigating a botched rescue

to free a kidnapped student, scion to a shoe
         empire; the driver, a former foot soldier,
former houseboy of a former general.
Someone is burning trash in the back lot.
     The old woman hikes up a cloudy day-

bed where smoke climbs, scumbles
         with the airwaves broadcasting a voice
you'd know, speaking in a murmur
inside a bus of yawning strangers,
         a bus sluicing through the fog

and along the economies, past lots
         and abandoned strip malls, a bus—
its radio loud, ascending toward cooler climes
where on a sunlit corner of the kitchen
         a radio is on for company to sleeping cats.

ON THE SORROWFUL FATHER STANDING. AND FALLING.

Everything is transparent. To look past
                   the surface is how I regard the father.
Stabilizing father . . . *stabat pater*,

the sorrowful father standing.
                   And falling. I loved the man for
having stayed, forgave him
                   when he strayed. He always

came home to us; in us he found
                   a home, though he
wasn't one for uniforms.

          How I esteem his sense of surfaces. His
cunning way of masking his gifts. Each day
                   turns into lines I am waiting to write.

Less conflicted, less estranged, not less
          lonely than when I arrived. I have located
a corner for myself. Arrival is a way of surfacing.

          Scuffing this trodden floor,
a dancehall jig dissecting the familiar
          from the strange. I've seen him hide
in the facets of a semiprecious stone.

"This is how it must feel to be you."
     See the fallen pink petals in a heap.
So many pink petals gathered on the street.
        Women in colorful scarves meet after work.

They brush by like wind-jostled branches,
      petals scurry like snow. One lands
on the lunar landscape of a bald man's head.

STONE

Her coffin looked like a gaudy purse
pink, extraterrestrial, yet sublime
                              a storyteller

who understands control
        of the what & where
to plant her feet for emphasis & know when
        to gad about lightly

        When you decided to abandon all
directives for persuasion, you agreed that stone
        is that thing uttered when all is lost

Mania is the mother
of all your best decisions amid the sanity
        of earth & grass, creeping & bent
because stone is not related to anything

A stone is a stone is a heart
                in your suit of hearts
an arresting melody you just know

When you call to ask whether he's decided
        on a tie to wear, be mindful of his state
of unintended denials

Harden yourself when reminding him
        that his wife will be buried the next day
There will be a long pause

Then he'll thank you for the heads-up
    In this way he can be stone-faced
when he sees the other people at her funeral

GHOST CAR

[*The dress she wanted to wear*]

A scent pressed like thumbprints on file folders,
On the mouthpiece of the phone cradled on her desk.
It was her perfume that would seep and linger.

She struggled with the tasks of applying foundation,
Eyeliner, and lipstick kept in a zippered bag,
Essentials she held on to like a lifeline.

Her daughters huddled round her bed
Before she died, waited for a weighty truth

She wanted to unburden, a revelation,
Or confession, a final appraisal of her life.
But what she left them were instructions.

[*From the open casket: a ball gown—the dress*]

What more is there, but only the appearance of things?
She wanted to be dressed with butterfly wing sleeves
And her matching shoes; her wig done right.

When her condition worsened, you tell her
That you do not care for visits from the afterlife.
She absorbs your plea like a pathogen
Greets a host, once revealed; unfolds
In the way dim lamps on a quiet lane
Blossom just before breaking into full light.

[Hospital beds turn into mattress-graves]

When you see your mother feeding only on oxygen,
You tell your sister about the smell of rose water—
Her scent in your bedroom 3,000 miles away.

Your sister relays the story to your mother
On the last day she saw her alive—
Recalls how your mother laughed and laughed

Even when laughing and breathing was hard—.
Like laughter rising to an aria, resonant,
An immigrant's final act sung with longing and hope.

She boards a car pungent with rose water
Where your father, a ghost, lives in a city no longer
His city, and drives a car that's no longer his car.

TO THE WIFE, AN ODE

On the night of Arturo Gatti's death, he and his wife
had a nasty fight outside a bar. Witnesses say
a man stepped in when he started hitting his wife.

Gatti pummeled the man with his ungloved hand
for interfering.   What I know
about marriage is about as much
as I know about boxing: you have to go

the distance even after you get knocked down.
"A light hand" doesn't translate well
in my mother's language. A man with a light hand
will beat his wife. And if you ask the wife,

she will tell you that a great fight demands
more than a quick hand. Great fights end in knockouts.

The wife was arrested for homicide, but was released
after Gatti's autopsy ruled that he died of suicide.

> [*Things the wife carries in her purse*]
> plaster of paris
> glue stick
> amaryllis
> receipt from Wo Loy Goy
> Friday night
> shiv

It's the sweet talk she punctuates with *emoji*.
[*I'll cut you. I'll make you bleed. Wink.*]

I dream of Gatti still living
and feeding on figs and ghost food.

Once I heard the wife singing, the last
lion to her pride. Baby lions clubbing their paws
on each other's heads.
Such was her brief history of happiness.

THE BOY LAZARUS

hoarded his sentences
     like wadded bills in a jar
in a house three sisters deep
     One day he found his tongue

and said: It's the elsewhere god
     I cannot fathom. The house
with his sisters stayed the same
     despite his new phobia

for flames. What was that field
     he asked his sister Magda
where all the souls had gathered
     Because he had to die

then was called back to life
     you'd think he'd have more to say
For him death was like oversleeping
     And waking was worse

with all these strands
     of cobwebby questions like why
couldn't Jesus just let him be
     Oh sure, he was needed

around his sisters' house, the fence
     required mending, the oxcart
wheel was busted. Who rotated
     with his sisters on market day

Death, if anything, gave the boy Lazarus
        meaning, even though he mostly
moped around all day
        He dreamt of a lost silence

with no sisters going on and on
        about their cousin changing water
into wine, making the lame
        walk *blah, blah, blah*

It was better being dead
        though he knew he couldn't say it
Why couldn't Jesus
        pick up a broom once in a while
or at least take out the trash

SHALL WE MEET AT THE LITTLE LAMBS?

Ragdale House

Midway on our long drive up north
      it came to pass the night before last
how dreams collapse
      into one tectonic plate
against another and heap into a strange
      garland strung by fault lines,

as is often the case in midlife,
      a string of pearls we've strung,
one clean sentence to the next

unraveling into homely phrases.
      Seeing you at the end of our travels
is how Dante opens
      with the pilgrim in an alien forest—

looking for beauty in her footprints,
      moving and not moving
as silent beings in a haunted landscape.

This compulsion, this ghost greed,
      this giving over, a discourse of bleeding

utterances, though that shouldn't disturb anyone
      posting his manhood indiscriminately on
the worldwide wreckage of ten thousand "likes."
      Anonymous consort, I am yours!

And you, player, who choose only winners,
as in the story of the pilgrim whose fugitive
        possessions morph into a long caravan

of unremarkable crèches except for the little lambs,
        meek as St. Agnes offering herself to the fire.

What does it matter, knowing the origins
        of the moony craters far above the lake
when you're falling in a well deep as debt,
        or deep as trouble, or deep as breath?

A PSALM FOR BEAUTY AND VIOLENCE

Just playing rough, / like young America will. —Derek Walcott

I splayed the book open and the spine cracked and the pages fell away. Reminds me of my beating when I was fourteen. Had just woken from a long nap—my head still lagging in a blissful bog. Me all up in my tall heels we called "platforms" with my popinjay shirt and flared bell-bottoms crossing the street, lord, oh lord, have mercy on this fool on his way to a beatdown. A carload of white boys was speeding up the street, not minding me strutting like a jaybird on the crosswalk. They honked instead of stopping. I stopped and let them by but flipped them off. Thought that was that. Then the car came to a halt and one boy jumped out and clocked me. I was down; and the other three or four came out and started kicking my sides, my hands covering my face. I took a licking like a Timex watch. You figure them boys didn't get much love where they lived. I dusted the footprints from my shirt and pants the way one beats an old rug to retain its beauty. / . . . / Amid rows and rows of beautiful houses, there was a neighborhood where a white boy smacked me in the face and kicked me several times when I was on the ground. And a brown boy, who avenged my beating, who sought out the other boys and beat them with fists and baseball bat, is now dead from a heart attack; dead on the green lawn he just mowed. Greenness spreading like a rumor, opening within us a dormant space for a little song for this patch of lawn pressed by his weight—his jaw slackened, a cool blade of grass lips the brute hour of his final day.

YO-YO BOY

It was a fever that made the yo-yo—
a brushfire in the homelands.
But a man who calls another a yo-yo
might as well say *tookas* instead of *ass*.

Now a good yo-yo is hard to find.
And a good man who can master
the craft of string and a pair of joined discs
[I'm talking about the old plastic kind

with a Coca-Cola logo on both sides]
deserves all the honors he is heir to.
So sue me for longing for a place
I never inhabited. Sue me for being

a hobgoblin of a diminished empire,
as my uncle Pedro "The Sleeper" Flores
loves to say at our family gatherings.
Uncle Flo is no match for the young bucks

like the trick-master chump from Chico
who crushed the Prague competition
with his overtly complex string moves,
or Baby Suzuki from Tokyo

with his menacing stealth and speed:
his yo-yo could literally take out an eye.
I'd give my eyetooth for just one of his tricks.
It's a young man's game like anything else.

So I say *tookas* to my rocking-the-cradle,
tookas for my walking-the-dog,
tookas for Pedro "The Sleeper" Flores
and his yo-yo that set the world on fire.

[All-American Alien]

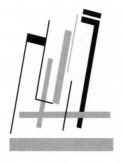

SALT SONG

Known to salt away his income, my brother-in-law
enters the walled city with a spooky Latin name:
Aigues-Mortes, the place of dead waters
where anonymous tourists depart with salt
in urnlike canisters bearing the ashes

of ephemeral bodies we return to sea.
Bird-haunted promenades near the sea
bear men who've had run-ins with the law.
Smoked Newports, this one & flicked ashes
on our carpet, so Dick became his nickname

because that's what he was to some whose salt
was worth the skin of any cod out of water.
What I meant by that last remark with water
was that every Dick has a future in the sea
of which the dead turned over in their beds of salt.

Such is the story of Aigues-Mortes & the law
of supply & demand, a Dick by any other name
like his brown brother who farmed the marshes
before starting a band that covered "Ashes to Ashes"
by an astronaut junkie floating in the blue waters—

that final frontier Houston called by another name
like apple is to gravity & waves are to the sea.
Time was & time when even my brother-in-law
believed that he was a true salt-of-the-earth
believer from the avenues where salt

from tears reduced men to scrims of ashes.
In cane fields & canneries, my brother-in-law
always had his guitar to serenade the water—
twangy tunes with grit about men lost at sea
who promised to give some girl their name.

His songs were corny, so they had names
like lonely Dick songs for sour milk & salty.
I think of him while driving out to the sea,
cradling the *fleur de sel* like an urn of ashes.
He hurled his past in the bay's oily waters—

blessings for fugitive voices down by law.
Brother, may our names be writ like law
on water & salt be our only measure.
Let the sea inherit these our scattered ashes.

ALL-AMERICAN ALIEN BOY

What was I then, but a dwarf of myself
in those canvas spats and kerchief

Boy with motto, boy in short khaki
boy with pocketknife and compass

boy with wood shop nunchucks
boy with elephant whistle ring

boy with tree-branch slingshot
boy disunited with himself

That it was a white hanky
his father owned and the boy

had taken to raise his new flag
Our patrol was called Charlie

Our scout leader owned a ham radio
Our flag was tied to a branch

We bivouacked along the tide pool
mussels bound by byssal threads

on wave-pummeled rocks   We
scraped the mussels from the rocks

dumped them in a pot to rinse
Who bothered to bring the pot

Haul ginger root and garlic cloves
Who brought the pot for rice

Over the fire blue shells opened
like genitalia in Sex Ed class

Broth from mussel brine juices
with ginger and sluiced salt

and our patrol leader waving
our new flag from a distance

hoo-ha hoo-ha hoo-ha-ha
singing *Standing by the highway* . . .

Ain't no fun to me
And me, not yet a man but an oath

a recitation, looming amid the rocks
gnomic and nine, backed by sun

an emanation from the sea
the boy I was (swear it!) was a god

ON THE GUTTURAL SONG OF MACHINES

1.

    Around the time of Sister Mary Emerentiana, a careless
    slip of the phrase *a lot* would be backhanded
    with arcane fact: "A lot is 700 x 1,200 square feet."

She suffered from rosacea, which blossomed
    as bruising on her cheeks. The pained concentration
of a hen laying an egg was her one expression,

framed by the starched armor of her habit,
even when relating to us her mundane tasks

transmuted into the guttural songs
    of machines making hay on Market Street,

where nuns comforted the victims of the 1906
    earthquake and for which the Sisters
of the Presentation were granted

    the privilege of paying only a nickel to ride
the bus in perpetuity. It was a story she clung to
    like pretty lies we dole out to innocents.

On Market and Powell she took her lunch
    at the Woolworth's counter of tuna fish
sandwich with a cup of black coffee.

    Such was the texture of memory: how a lot
is etherealized into an elderly woman in a habit
alone at a lunch counter downtown.

2.
I want to see beyond the lot I've inherited—
        frustrated by the body trapped by its skin.

This rash on Sister Mary Emerentiana's cheeks
        spread like a map of rebellious pigmentation.

In another time when the Church had inveigled
        a diocese of illiterates—it relied on music

as its bread and butter. In Fela Kuti's Africa
        "Shuffering and Shmiling" embodied

                consciousness and commotion—
so far so far so far for what / na your fault to be that.
On my front porch bordering America,

        we're passing around the recreational smoke
and taking a mighty hit of the "Communio:

Lux Aeterna, Cum Sanctis Tuis" from Mozart's
        Requiem: time, as it tends to do, slows down
to an astonishing stillness the way

a hummingbird's frenzied speech lasts
        as long as a beloved's embrace, or as one
slips into the body of her better self.

FAILURE

I think I will do nothing now
but listen. Listen and rest
my head on the noise of familiars.
To accrue what I hear into myself
and let the pitter-patter,
the birdy chatter, the *kokoro* of the core,
or the ta Dum, ta Dum ta . . .
accumulate in me.

How Hopkins does it,
holds us captive—I cannot tell—.
Or how Pessoa makes us
forget how to spell . . .

Today I felt like a failure,
a harangue bird whose calls jolt
like a doorbell, or smother
like a peacoat in summer.

My malarkey is no more
No mas talky talky por mio.
For I know failure well.
I live in her house and make her bed.

Serve her tea and toast
and sweep up her mess—.
You can say she's harsh,
but she's also a kind master,
whispering the infinite
in my ear when I choose to listen.

SALT

Some meals are better seen than eaten
Sentences better
mangled than diagrammed

Life for you must be easy   because you are beautiful
Because one day   in a white cave
in a far-off mountain   weeks after you elected to burn

your daughters will be plying jorums of liquor
to dull your husband's senses for good measure
Your girls and their odd instinct

for procreation will do what they must
to repopulate this plain of ash

Sea salt with mouth slightly ajar—
plain beauty with jaunty scarf
My American high school Spanish
no clearer than my butchered
French diagrammed as hieroglyphs
on a street in a distant country
Most days it's all about the brag
an onlooker to your own disaster

I turned to stone
Me who ran among the lesser adjectives
in a city of better nouns

MY LANKY, LANDLOCKED SO-AND-SO

In my recent past, I was an Indiana
Our present business is
loving an Indiana   I'm going abroad

I told my professor   "What's her name?"
he asked   My uptake then was slow
I was that, but I'm now, not an Indiana

If I come back, I won't ever owe
a nickel to Indiana; each month my bank
will tally a tidy sum for my depositaries

"Someone's gonna get this dollar," man
                said to the porter
Come back to Indiana—not too late!

It's only the plentiful all-grabbing sky
And when four and twenty blackbirds

began to bake into a pie in Indiana
wasn't that a Dixie Chopper who cried
"Never, never, never, never, never!"

before the fool in iambic pentameter?
And princes astride their mowers
barebacked to sun their hides and bake

before the king   So many birds
will black out the sun in Indiana—
I am that and my threats of return

FRONTIER PSYCHIATRY

I won't sleep for another six days.
Each day for the rest of the week will be
a workday, buckle down, catch-up week.
The election of 2016 has left me jumpy.
I've dialed back on serious attention,
I've dialed back on trusting neighbors.
God, or this brutal season ending
in spring snow, has Her special malice
despite the full-throated birds singing
in the eaves.   Forty years ago,
I had a morning paper route I began
at 5:00 a.m. and completed by 6:00,
or sometimes 6:30. I'm remembering
this with the cold nipping my ankles
and the smoky coolness of the air
outside my window.   I was angry
at my mother that particular morning.
We had fought about something
I no longer remember. It was a Saturday
and I had just finished my paper route
and I didn't want to go home. I saw
light emanating from the lone diner
in our neighborhood. Big Joe's Grill
was terra incognita for a boy my age
where older men with gray fedoras
would sit with a cup of black coffee
and a slice of apple pie; a greasy spoon
with chrome and red swivel chairs.
Big Joe was a short Asian man
with a clean white apron and an

extended arm directing me to sit down.
I didn't know what I wanted, or why
I even bothered entering his place.
But once inside I felt at ease,
an understated sense of joy, or
what goodness must feel like after
a long, difficult journey.   Joe
must have read the fierce loneliness
on my face before I could open my mouth.
I was a boy with only so many words,
though my face was an open book. Then
I remembered to check my pockets
for money and fished out a buck
and some loose change. Maybe $1.50.
"Don't worry about it,"
was the first thing he said to me.
"You want eggs?" he asked.
I nodded and I watched him break
two and slap down a hamburger patty
on the hot griddle. Maybe he saw me
as a stray, a boy on the outs with his family.
He served the eggs and the patty
and some buttered toast with
a blend of dignity and disdain—
what I understood later when thinking
of my mother's own form of grace.
Immigrant begets immigrant,
our departure begets constant arrival.
I know now just enough of what I
inherited and what I will leave to air.

ODE

I can hear the pregnant woman behind me,
       rooting an unconvincing cheer.
How pleasing, her birdlike voice, her half-

       hearted cry, her affliction, a half heart,
her faint rabbit reveille.
       And because of the rain and César Vallejo

in Paris writing his human poems, Vallejo
       looking at the rain and seeing
only black stones on white stones falling

       on the street and it is already Thursday.
In October, on a day much like today when
       the husband of the pregnant woman

would no longer remember the roar in his chest
when he and his pregnant wife
       had pledged allegiance to dim hope—

in the sad refrain of dual citizenship
with all the heady hail in his ball cap,
his juiced hurrahs. Tonight I dissolve

       in perpetual displacement,
recall our pennant chant with my one
good ear as if to say I am here now,

I bought the farm and I'm not leaving—
      in spite of history,
in spite of my flat Malay nose,

        and the broken elegies
for my poet Vallejo dying in the rain.

BABY AMERICAN

There are no duty-free catalogs on this trip,
no declaration cards for immigration, no in-flight mags
with ads for steakhouses in Dallas, Cincinnati,
or Indianapolis, no pleasing stewards in pressed blazers
pushing beverage carts,
no first class, or pretzels, no one puts on any airs,
or tells you, please buckle up
and lift your trays in their secure and locked positions.
The terminal where you wait before boarding
has a busy security guard who speaks a language
other than your own. He runs
a tight ship and lets you know who's in charge.
Though no one cares.
The ammonia fumes from the bathroom tell you
the terminal is spick-and-span,
at least at this hour when anytime is the right time
to troll for porn,
so *sayeth* that dude two seats down with his laptop.

A bearded backpacker snoozes
with security rousing him to check for his bus ticket.
There are no hoboes
here even though everyone here is homeless.
It's just a question of degree.
On the TV monitor is a CNN story about a woman in a hijab
suing an employer for discrimination.
An army-jacketed man makes his displeasure known
regarding the merits of her suit.
Nobody's ever guaranteed a job—loud enough for all to hear.

I stare at the mirrored view of the oncoming traffic
but not the trees racing by me.
We've journeyed westward for days on what feels
like the slowest train to Calcutta.
This isn't a transpacific voyage—
home is just beyond the next stop.
We're solitude-in-transit, a virus coursing
through a difficult vein.
This is no joyride, no freedom riders here.
This bus isn't bound for Selma, but to Seaside, Astoria,
and clear up to Tacoma.

At the strip mall where the bus stops, a couple
in their twenties with a homely child disembarks.
From our window we watch like yawning neighbors
taking stock of the family next door
unloading their U-Haul truck.
The hold below contained their nary precious stuff:

why two chain locks for the bike?
Stroller for baby, her plastic tub, too, oversized backpacks,
and several plastic bags for wares and whatnot.

My feelings weren't bulletproof, so I wondered if they
were happy and decided later the way
politicians regard their constituents as happy after all.
Across the street was the ARCO station
and in front of the mall

was a giant sign: KARATE, GUNS & TANNING—
another banner year for guns and gardens,
our arsenal democracy, our ruin porn.

Notes

"Implicit Body": "Call me Mr. Gone / who's done made / some other plans" is from Stevie Wonder's song "Maybe Your Baby." The actual line is, "Maybe your baby done made some other plans."

"Zones of Contact": *Enter several strange Shapes* is from *The Tempest*, Act III, Scene III.

"Apron": *Mon coeur mis à nu* (*my heart laid bare*) is a line from Baudelaire.

"The Shape Of" is from Jorge Luis Borges's short story "The Form of the Sword."

"Why They Bees That Way" is for Garrett Hongo.

"The Maid" is a Golden Shovel exercise from Gwendolyn Brooks's "Bronzeville Woman in a Red Hat."

"My Phantom Escort, Pier Paolo Pasolini" is from *Roman Nights and Other Stories* by Pasolini.

"Sightseer in This Killing City": The line "On things asleep, no balm" is from Roethke's poem "The Longing."

"Ave Nacirema": "And the sheen of their spears . . ." is from "The Destruction of Sennacherib" by Lord Byron.

"Like the Spars of a Sailing Ship": "There is only the trying. The rest . . ." is from "East Coker" in *Four Quartets* by T. S. Eliot.

"The War on Drugs": The line "that men are as the time is" is from *King Lear*, Act V, Scene III.

"All-American Alien Boy": "Standing by the highway" is from Al .93. Green's song "It Ain't No Fun to Me."

"Failure": *I think I will do nothing now but listen, / To accrue what I hear into myself* are lines from Walt Whitman.

"My Lanky, Landlocked So-and-So": "Come back to Indiana— not too late!" is from Hart Crane's "Indiana," and "Never, never, never, never, never!" is from *King Lear*, Act V, Scene III.

"Frontier Psychiatry" is in memory of Philip Levine.

The name "Nacirema" comes from artist Michael Arcega's clever use of nomenclature as a way of examining Filipino American identity as well as his repurposing of Horace Miner's essay "Body Ritual Among the Nacirema," from *American Anthropologist*, 1956.

Acknowledgments

The American Poetry Review: "Baby American," "The Pall of a Past World," and "Salt"

Bellingham Review: "All-American Alien Boy" and "The War on Drugs"

Boulevard: "Ave Nacirema"

Cavalier Literary Couture: "The Boy Lazarus" (as "Lazarus")

Cimarron Review: "Zones of Contact"

Drunken Boat: "Alfonso Street"

The Hampden-Sydney Poetry Review: "The Suitcase"

Harvard Review: "Nighthawks Oceania"

Kenyon Review: "In the Andes"

Memorious: "Failure" and "Nurse Nacirema"

Oxford Magazine: "The Monk's Tale" (as "Death and the Barber")

Poetry Northwest: "On the Gutteral Song of Machines"

Prairie Schooner: "Yo-Yo Boy" (as "The Yo-Yo Heir's Lament")

Shenandoah: "Apron"

Tongue: A Journal of Writing & Art: "Liner Notes for Monk"

TriQuarterly: "The Holler"

"Alfonso Street" appeared in *Not Like the Rest of Us: An Anthology of Contemporary Indiana Writers*, edited by Barbara Shoup and Rachel Sahaidachny.

"Alfonso Street" also appeared in *Union: 15 Years of Drunken Boat / 50 Years of Writing from Singapore*, edited by Alvin Pang and Ravi Shankar.

"Liner Notes for Monk" appeared in *The Best American Poetry: 2014*, guest-edited by Terrance Hayes.

"The Maid" appeared in *The Golden Shovel Anthology: New Poems Honoring Gwendolyn Brooks*, edited by Peter Kahn, Ravi Shankar, and Patricia Smith.

I am grateful to Willapa Bay AiR, the MacDowell Colony, Montalvo Arts Center, Djerassi Resident Artists Program, the Virginia Center for the Creative Arts, VCCA-France, and the Ragdale Foundation for the time and space that allowed me to write many of the poems in this collection. I also want to thank DePauw University for the Martha C. Rieth Faculty Fellowship and other awards, and for the inspiration I draw from my colleagues, friends, and students.

Many thanks to these generous souls for their encouragement: Henry Louis Gates Jr., Garrett Hongo, Karen Long, Terrance Hayes, Yona Harvey, Robert Wrigley, Corrinne Hales, Li-Young Lee, Rigoberto González, Yusef Komunyakaa, David Mura, Marilyn Chin, Jennifer Chang, Natalie Diaz, Anna Rose Welch, Sarah Gambito, Joseph Legaspi, Luisa Igloria, Daniel Chacón, Michelle Naka Pierce, Keith Tuma, Fidelito Cortes, Nerissa Balce, Cristina Pantoja Hidalgo, Patrick Rosal, Gémino Abad, Luis Francia, Midori Yamamura, Eric Gamalinda, Marnie McInnes, my family and friends in the Bay Area (Kirstie, Yvette, Larry, Aris, Ditas, Joey, Baby, Richard, Annette, Ray, and Corette), and the Singson family in the Detroit area and Chicago.

Special thanks to Paul Slovak for his guidance and support over the years, and to Karen Singson, whose love makes everything possible.

AMBER BOWERS

Eugene Gloria's previous poetry collections are *My Favorite Warlord* (2012), winner of the Anisfield-Wolf Book Award; *Hoodlum Birds* (2006); and *Drivers at the Short-Time Motel* (2000), a National Poetry Series selection and recipient of the Asian American Literary Award.

PENGUIN POETS

PAIGE ACKERSON-
KIELY
*Dolefully, A Rampart
Stands*

JOHN ASHBERY
Selected Poems
*Self-Portrait in a Convex
Mirror*

PAUL BEATTY
Joker, Joker, Deuce

JOSHUA BENNETT
The Sobbing School

TED BERRIGAN
The Sonnets

LAUREN BERRY
The Lifting Dress

JOE BONOMO
Installations

PHILIP BOOTH
*Lifelines: Selected Poems
1950–1999*
Selves

JIM CARROLL
*Fear of Dreaming:
The Selected Poems*
Living at the Movies
Void of Course

ALISON HAWTHORNE
DEMING
Genius Loci
Rope
Stairway to Heaven

CARL DENNIS
Another Reason
Callings
*New and Selected Poems
1974–2004*
Night School
Practical Gods
Ranking the Wishes
Unknown Friends

DIANE DI PRIMA
Loba

STUART DISCHELL
Backwards Days
Dig Safe

STEPHEN DOBYNS
*Velocities: New and
Selected Poems:
1966–1992*

EDWARD DORN
Way More West

ROGER FANNING
The Middle Ages

ADAM FOULDS
The Broken Word

CARRIE FOUNTAIN
Burn Lake
Instant Winner

AMY GERSTLER
Crown of Weeds
Dearest Creature
Ghost Girl
Medicine
Nerve Storm
Scattered at Sea

EUGENE GLORIA
*Drivers at the
Short-Time Motel*
Hoodlum Birds
My Favorite Warlord
*Sightseer in This
Killing City*

DEBORA GREGER
By Herself
*Desert Fathers,
Uranium Daughters*
God
In Darwin's Room
*Men, Women, and
Ghosts*
Western Art

TERRANCE HAYES
*American Sonnets for My
Past and Future Assassin*
Hip Logic
How to Be Drawn
Lighthead
Wind in a Box

NATHAN HOKS
The Narrow Circle

ROBERT HUNTER
Sentinel and Other Poems

MARY KARR
Viper Rum

WILLIAM KECKLER
Sanskrit of the Body

JACK KEROUAC
Book of Blues
Book of Haikus
Book of Sketches

JOANNA KLINK
Circadian
*Excerpts from a
Secret Prophecy*
Raptus

JOANNE KYGER
As Ever: Selected Poems

ANN LAUTERBACH
Hum
*If in Time: Selected Poems,
1975–2000*
On a Stair
Or to Begin Again
Spell
Under the Sign

CORINNE LEE
Plenty
Pyx

PHILLIS LEVIN
May Day
Mercury
*Mr. Memory & Other
Poems*

PENGUIN POETS

PATRICIA LOCKWOOD
*Motherland Fatherland
  Homelandsexuals*

WILLIAM LOGAN
Macbeth in Venice
Madame X
Rift of Light
Strange Flesh
The Whispering Gallery

J. MICHAEL MARTINEZ
Museum of the Americas

ADRIAN MATEJKA
The Big Smoke
Map to the Stars
Mixology

MICHAEL MCCLURE
*Huge Dreams: San Francisco
  and Beat Poems*

ROSE MCLARNEY
Its Day Being Gone

DAVID MELTZER
*David's Copy: The Selected
  Poems of David Meltzer*

ROBERT MORGAN
Dark Energy
Terroir

CAROL MUSKE-DUKES
Blue Rose
An Octave Above Thunder
Red Trousseau
Twin Cities

ALICE NOTLEY
Certain Magical Acts
Culture of One
The Descent of Alette
Disobedience
In the Pines
Mysteries of Small Houses

WILLIE PERDOMO
The Crazy Bunch
*The Essential Hits of
  Shorty Bon Bon*

LIA PURPURA
*It Shouldn't Have Been
  Beautiful*

LAWRENCE RAAB
The History of Forgetting
Visible Signs

BARBARA RAS
The Last Skin
One Hidden Stuff

MICHAEL ROBBINS
Alien vs. Predator
The Second Sex

PATTIANN ROGERS
Generations
Holy Heathen Rhapsody
Quickening Fields
Wayfare

SAM SAX
Madness

ROBYN SCHIFF
A Woman of Property

WILLIAM STOBB
Absentia
Nervous Systems

TRYFON TOLIDES
*An Almost Pure
  Empty Walking*

SARAH VAP
Viability

ANNE WALDMAN
Gossamurmur
Kill or Cure
Manatee/Humanity
*Structure of the World
  Compared to a Bubble*
Trickster Feminism

JAMES WELCH
Riding the Earthboy 40

PHILIP WHALEN
Overtime: Selected Poems

ROBERT WRIGLEY
*Anatomy of Melancholy and
  Other Poems*
Beautiful Country
Box
*Earthly Meditations:
  New and Selected Poems*
Lives of the Animals
Reign of Snakes

MARK YAKICH
*The Importance of Peeling
  Potatoes in Ukraine*
Spiritual Exercises
*Unrelated Individuals
  Forming a Group Waiting
  to Cross*